IMAGES
of America

DELAWARE WATER GAP
NATIONAL RECREATION AREA

Considered one of the natural wonders of the world in the 17th and 18th centuries, the Delaware Water Gap is the southern gateway to the Delaware Water Gap National Recreation Area, which extends north from the gap for the next 40 miles in both Pennsylvania and New Jersey. (Courtesy of the National Park Service.)

On the cover: The coming of the railroad had the biggest impact on transportation and trade in the upper Delaware River valley. By 1847, the first trains had reached Port Jervis, adding Newton, Sussex, and Franklin by 1871. In 1882, the New York, Susquehanna and Western Railroad ran from Weehawken to Stroudsburg, crossing the river just north of the present Route 80 toll bridge. (Courtesy of the National Park Service.)

IMAGES
of America

DELAWARE WATER GAP
NATIONAL RECREATION AREA

Laura Obiso

ARCADIA
PUBLISHING

Published by Arcadia Publishing
Charleston SC, Chicago IL, Portsmouth NH, San Francisco CA

Printed in the United States of America

Library of Congress Catalog Card Number: 2007932667

For all general information contact Arcadia Publishing at:
Telephone 843-853-2070
Fax 843-853-0044
E-mail sales@arcadiapublishing.com
For customer service and orders:
Toll-Free 1-888-313-2665

Visit us on the Internet at www.arcadiapublishing.com

This book is dedicated to the free-flowing Delaware River
and all the caretakers, past, present, and future,
who preserve and protect it as a wild and scenic place.

CONTENTS

Acknowledgments   6

Introduction   7

1.   People of the Minisink   9

2.   Frontier Life   13

3.   Wars, Forts, and Yaugh Houses   19

4.   From Settlement to Community   25

5.   Agriculture and Industry   45

6.   Boats, Trains, and Automobiles   65

7.   The Resort Era   77

8.   Flood, Fear, and Fiasco   97

9.   Recreation Area   111

ACKNOWLEDGMENTS

My thanks go to the National Park Service and the Delaware Water Gap National Recreation Area (DWGNRA) for their cooperation in compiling this book. Special thanks must be given to Susan Kopczynski, DWGNRA cultural resource specialist, who was instrumental in locating photographs and whose knowledge of historical information about the park is unsurpassed. Special thanks goes to Tom Solon, historic architect for the DWGNRA, for his assistance and photographs concerning restorations in the park. Thanks also to Michelle Jacques at the DWGNRA headquarters in Bushkill for knowing just where to look through thousands of photographs to find the ones I needed. Special thanks to Alicia Batko, Montague historian, and the members of the Montague Association for Restoration and Community History for their enthusiasm for this project. Thanks to Patte Haggerty Frato, Sandyston Township historian, whose family origins in Sandyston have given her an outstanding knowledge of local history. Thanks to my dear friend Casey Kays, who first introduced me to Sunfish Pond so long ago.

Erin Rocha, my editor at Arcadia Publishing, was a pleasure to worth with, always professional, prompt, and quick to respond to my questions.

Thanks are also in order for all those who offered memories, anecdotes, and recollections about the events that transpired over the years, including people who knew people that provided an extra story or photograph. Thanks to Carol Valotta for proofreading, Cheryl Geveke for recognizing my passionate feelings about this area and offering encouragement, Bob Socha for stopping at the Yellow Cottage to bring sandwiches and cannoli, and my mother, who kept asking, "When are you going to write another book?"

And finally, my heartfelt appreciation to my son Rob Socha, professional photographer and all-around nice guy, who took most of the present-day photographs and patiently answered frantic questions about pictures, computer scanners, and how technical and mechanical things work.

If I have missed anyone by name, I apologize. The brain may not have remembered, but the heart has not forgotten your kindness and cooperation. Thank you.

INTRODUCTION

The Delaware Water Gap National Recreation Area (DWGNRA) was created in 1965 to manage the recreational facilities and opportunities surrounding a 40-mile-long reservoir that would result from damming the Delaware River at Tocks Island. The dam would flood 23,000 acres of the upper Delaware River valley from a point just north of the Delaware Water Gap almost to Port Jervis, New York—an area known since the 1600s as the Minisink. The project was the brainchild of the Army Corps of Engineers.

The Lenape (pronounced Len-AH-pay) people were living, hunting, fishing, and farming the fertile valley when the first Dutch explorers and settlers arrived in the 1600s. For the most part, the Lenapes and the Europeans that settled in the valley enjoyed a peaceful coexistence, until the Lenapes realized that their home territories were becoming smaller and smaller. The infamous Walking Purchase of 1737 was the major event that set hostilities in motion.

By the time of the French and Indian War and the American Revolution, a series of forts had been constructed through the Minisink. Headquarters was located near the Isaac VanCampen Inn, a yaugh house on the Old Mine Road. John Adams, Gen. Horatio Gates, Benedict Arnold, and Count Casimir Pulaski were among the more notable people who spent the night at VanCampen's.

In the mid-1800s, people living in nearby cities in Pennsylvania and New Jersey discovered the unspoiled beauty and nature of the Delaware Water Gap. It was not long before nearly 40 hotels were built in the mountains and nearby towns. Landscape painters, naturalists, bird-watchers, botanists, actors and actresses, businessmen and their families, and even presidents came to relax in the natural beauty and wilderness. Many farmers catered to the needs of tourists by providing room and board during the summer tourist season.

In 1955, one of the worst and deadliest floods in the nation's history struck the Delaware valley. People started speaking up about flood control, and the Army Corps of Engineers targeted the Delaware River. They theorized that a dam would also provide drinking water and hydroelectric power for growing distant cities. The Tocks Island dam was authorized by Pres. John F. Kennedy in 1962 and included the creation of a Tocks Island Recreation Area to manage the facilities around the reservoir. The federal government began to acquire the homes and farms of valley residents, either by purchase or, for those really stubborn folks who refused to sell, by exercising the governmental right to eminent domain and seizure.

The idea of the Army Corps of Engineers did not fare well with activists who were already at work saving a small glacial lake on top of the mountain very close to Tocks Island. The fight to save Sunfish Pond, coupled with groups already forming to fight the dam, created a huge environmental movement in the upper Delaware River valley and started a political and environmental war that raged for decades.

In the wake of a massive environmental opposition, dwindling funds, and finally an unacceptable geological assessment for the safety of the dam, the push to build the Tocks Island dam waned. The government put the National Park Service in charge of the acquired properties. Instead of a reservoir, the area became the DWGNRA.

The National Park Service suddenly found itself the caretaker of hundreds of vacant historical houses that were not supposed to be there. For the park service, there followed many years of hard feelings and miserable failures, but it also managed to pull a few gems from the rubble of the Tocks Island fiasco.

In spite of its infamous beginnings, the DWGNRA is now a pristine, environmentally rich valley protecting the lands immediately adjacent to the wild and scenic Delaware River. Instead of condominiums and developments, there are 70,000 acres of managed wilderness, all within a short ride of the New York and Philadelphia metropolitan areas.

While it is impossible to tell the whole story of the DWGNRA in such a small space, it is hoped that the photographs and text will chronicle the life and times of this historic valley and the dam that nearly destroyed it forever. Future preservation depends on one's awareness of what took place here. It is hoped that this book will institute that awareness.

One

PEOPLE OF THE MINISINK

The Minisink was the name applied to about a 60-mile stretch of the Delaware River valley, from the Delaware Water Gap to about present-day Narrowsburg, New York. Where the Neversink River joins the Delaware River in Port Jervis, New York, the Delaware River makes a right-angle turn and flows southwest, parallel and immediately behind a ridge of mountains on the New Jersey side and with lesser mountains and ridges on the Pennsylvania side. The river makes a sharp S turn at Walpack Bend and continues its course to the water gap. At the Delaware Water Gap, the river again turns to the southeast and follows a less mountainous course to the Delaware Bay and Atlantic Ocean.

The Native Americans living in the Minisink area at the time the Europeans arrived were the Munsi Indians. From about the year 1600, the Lenape people lived throughout most of New Jersey and neighboring areas. Territory divided the Algonquin-speaking Lenapes into three groups, including the Unalachtigo Indians, living around Delaware Bay; the Unami Indians, living in central New Jersey; and the Munsi Indians (also written Munsee or Minsi), living in northern New Jersey and northeastern Pennsylvania. Later the English collectively called all these people Delawares, because of their proximity to the river. In the late 1600s, the Lenapes were loosely dominated by the more warlike Iroquois. Taking advantage of this social hierarchy, the Europeans called upon the Iroquois to persuade the reluctant Lenapes to leave the upper Delaware River valley in the years after the Walking Purchase of 1737.

Archaeological evidence shows that Paleo-Indians first inhabited the Minisink area almost 11,000 years ago after the retreat of the glacier that once covered the upper Delaware River valley. These people were nomadic hunters and gatherers who evolved into Woodland-period people and then finally into the more agriculturally minded Lenapes of the late-Woodland period. The Lenapes lived near and farmed the fertile river flatlands, planting beans, corn, and squash to supplement hunting and fishing. They built single-family homes of bent saplings covered with bark and larger longhouses for gatherings.

For the most part, the Lenapes coexisted peacefully with the European settlers until the fraudulent Walking Purchase resulted in hostility. Most of the Lenapes were driven from their homeland by the late 1700s.

The first people of the Minisink cultivated the rich floodplain of the Harry's farm site for at least two centuries. An archaeological excavation led by Dr. Herbert Kraft of the Seton Hall University museum was conducted in anticipation of the Tocks Island dam project. Over a period of several years, professional and amateur archaeologists assisted by volunteers of varying ages worked to carefully exhume the buried history of the first Minisink people. (Courtesy of the National Park Service.)

The Archaic period people who lived in the Minisink region came to the area nearly 11,000 years ago. No evidence of cooking pots or houses has been uncovered. These early people were nomadic, seeking shelter in rock outcroppings, and either ate meat raw or roasted it over an open fire. In contrast, many cooking pots, bowls, and evidence of more permanent houses of the late-Woodland period have been unearthed. (Courtesy of the National Park Service.)

Several house sites were uncovered in subsequent digs at the Harry's farm site. These people lived in single-family homes constructed of bent-over saplings covered with bark. The largest house uncovered measured 45 feet long and 17 feet wide and was situated about 80 feet from the river. At least one large storage pit was located inside the house, where the people stored dried fish, vegetables, dried meat, and other necessities. The storage pits were fairly large, some up to 48 inches deep and five or six feet in diameter. (Courtesy of the National Park Service.)

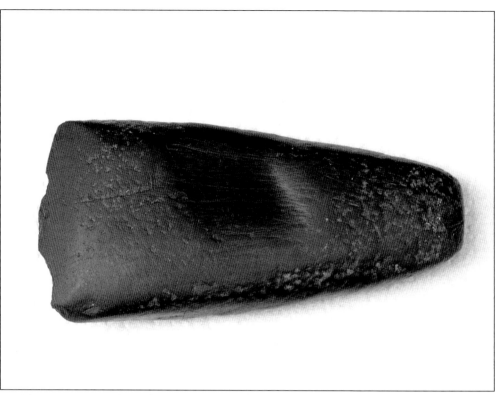

Archaeological excavations in the upper Delaware River valley uncovered many faces. Some were carved effigies (left), and others were imprinted on pottery pieces. It is generally thought that the Paleo-Indians entered the New Jersey and Pennsylvania areas around 10,500 to 8000 B.C. The polished stone celt (above) was discovered in the early 1960s on the river flats near Pahaquarry when about an inch of the small end was observed above ground. Such a tool was used to clean and scrape hides. An indentation has been etched into the surface, providing a more comfortable fit when grasping the stone, or perhaps the maker had something else in mind but never finished his creation. (Above, courtesy of Rob Socha; left, courtesy of the National Park Service.)

Two

FRONTIER LIFE

The Dutch were among the first Europeans in the upper Delaware River valley. They preferred to build stone houses, and by the 1700s, several of these structures were established along the river.

Obtaining land in the Delaware River valley was first accomplished through state-appropriated land grants to settlers. Colonial governments bargained with the Delawares to purchase land, a concept not fully understood by the Native Americans, who believed that no one could own land. In their understanding, they were granting hunting, fishing, and living rights to the Europeans to share the *use* of the land. They never expected to be forced to give up their own rights to use the land and certainly did not foresee that they would eventually be forced to leave their ancestral homelands.

The early settlers and the Delawares had a tolerable relationship until the infamous Walking Purchase of 1737. The sons of William Penn told the Delawares that Penn had made a treaty with them some 50 years before to obtain land in Pennsylvania. The Delawares did not remember the treaty, and so an agreement was made to sell the Penns as much land as could be walked in a day and a half northwest from Wrightstown. The Penns hired runners and altered the course of the walk so that in the end, they gained another 1,200 acres from the Delawares. After this event, attacks on settlements became more frequent.

By the mid-1700s, most of the remaining Delawares had left the upper Delaware River region, and the frontier opened up for European settlement. South of the water gap, most settlers arrived from Philadelphia. As more people came into the upper Delaware River valley, small villages and settlements began to appear.

Tedeuskund, recognized by the English as a leader of the Delawares, initiated the first Native American attacks on the Minisink settlements during the winter of 1755–1756, in part as retaliation for the Walking Purchase deception and also because of encouragement by the French to make war on the English settlers.

Here is a portrait of Lappawinsoe, one of the Lenape leaders who signed the infamous Walking Purchase of 1737. Gustavus Hesselius, noted as being the first artist in the New World to realistically capture the facial features of the Native Americans, painted this portrait in the 1700s. (Courtesy of the National Park Service.)

A View at Pahaquarra, Sussex County, New-Jersey.

One of the first illustrations of pioneer life was captured in this 1794 woodcut of Pahaquarra just north of the Delaware Water Gap. A similar engraving done by the same artist depicts early life in the Minisink region of New Jersey, showing early one-and-a-half-story cabins, Dutch-style barns, and wooden rail fencing. Both engravings appeared in 1794 issues of the *New Yorker* magazine. (Courtesy of the National Park Service.)

A View, at Minisink, New-Jersey.

The life of the pioneers in the upper Delaware River valley was difficult at best. The earliest cabins were most likely built of sawed or hewed logs and were small one- or two-room structures with a half-story space above. Chinking of mud, hair, paper, straw, and almost anything else that could be used for insulation was packed between the logs. Early cabins were similar to this one but lacked the glass windows and doors. Windows were closed with solid wood doors for protection against attack. (Courtesy of the Library of Congress, Prints and Photographs Division.)

Colonial Dutch settlers preferred one-and-a-half-story stone houses with a pitched gable roof. This solid little house, built by William Ennis is 1751, also has the eyebrow windows that seem to be a popular feature in early upper Delaware River valley houses. Ennis was one of the first schoolteachers in the upper Delaware River valley. (Courtesy of the National Park Service.)

In the earliest stone houses, cooking was done in the oversize fireplaces that also provided heat. Cast-iron pots hung from a metal crane that swung out toward the room for easy access. Another apparatus allowed pots to be raised or lowered over the fire. Most meals consisted of milk, cheese, freshly churned butter, eggs, salted pork, game, and vegetables from the garden. In the winter, vegetables stored in a root cellar were served boiled or stewed with salt pork or fresh game. Some farmhouses also had a summer kitchen—a detached fireplace or cooking area that kept the heat from cooking fires outside the main house. Larger houses often had a beehive oven next to the fireplace built into the wall of the house. A Colonial woman could judge the temperature of the beehive oven by how warm it felt to her hand, and she knew how to adjust the coals to change the baking temperatures. The ovens were cleaned by sweeping the ashes toward an opening at the front, which emptied into the fireplace. (Courtesy of the National Park Service.)

The early settlers of the upper Delaware River valley endured hardships and discomforts of everyday life that one cannot imagine today. The massive stone houses had no indoor plumbing or heating but were heated by fireplaces in every room. Cast-iron firebacks were placed on the back wall of the fireplace to reflect warmth into the room and to protect the wall from the excessive and constant heat. This fireback, made in the Oxford Furnace in Warren County and dated 1748, was discovered sealed up in one of the fireplaces in the VanCampen Inn during a remodeling by one of the former residents. It was later determined that the fireplace was used very little or not at all and was most likely sealed at an early date and replaced by a cast-iron Dutch five-plate stove. Stoves of this type were available in the New Jersey area by 1728. (Courtesy of the National Park Service.)

Three

WARS, FORTS, AND YAUGH HOUSES

The upper Delaware River valley played an important role in the French and Indian War and the American Revolution.

Early relationships with the Delaware Indians were tolerably friendly, and there was little need for fortifications in the upper Delaware River valley. After the Walking Purchase and in the years prior to the French and Indian War, the tone of the Lenapes changed, and matters worsened when the Lenapes were ordered by the dominant Iroquois to surrender their homelands to the Europeans.

When the French and Indian War broke out in 1754, many of the Native Americans that once lived in the upper Delaware River valley believed they might recover their lost lands by aligning with the French and returned to the Minisink to attack English settlers. A band led by Tedeuskund reportedly sought revenge for the Walking Purchase deception. Settlers on both sides of the Delaware River were raided, and their homes were burned.

A few of the Pennsylvania forts close to New Jersey provided protection for many New Jersey settlers, except for the stretch of river between the Delaware Water Gap and the New York border. Alarmed by increasing hostilities in 1756, the New Jersey Colonial government authorized the building of blockhouses, roughly following the Delaware River, to be manned by local militia. There are not many written records of these forts, but they are shown on a 1750s map.

Colonial law already called for the provision of yaugh houses, which stated that any house in a remote area was required to take in travelers needing shelter. The VanCampen Inn on the Old Mine Road in New Jersey was never an inn at all; it was a yaugh house. At one time during a Native American raid, 150 men, women, and children took shelter behind the 22-inch stone walls.

During the Revolutionary War, Gen. Horatio Gates and his aid Benedict Arnold marched with 600 troops down the Old Mine Road on their way to join George Washington in the battle of Trenton. They were caught in a blizzard in December 1776. Gates stayed at the VanCampen yaugh house, while the troops camped in the Shapanack flats across the road.

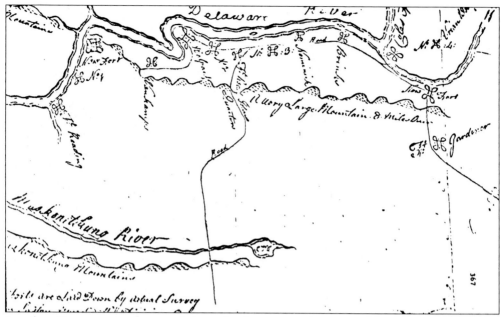

Jonathan Hampton, supply commissioner for the provincial troops in New Jersey, wrote a letter in May 1758 in which he mentioned a line of forts roughly following the Delaware River. "Our first Fort, Reading, is 12 miles above Easton, the 2nd Fort at Col. VanCampen's 18 miles further, to Fort Walpack 6, to Headquarters 6, to Nominack Fort 8, to Shipeconk Fort 4, to Cole's Fort 8, These on the Delaware River. Then to Fort Gardiner, below the Great Mountain, 12." Soon afterward, Hampton drew a map with some differences, including additional blockhouses and a mention of Fort Carmer being eight miles from Fort Nominack. The Minisink portion of Hampton's map is shown above. The small stone house pictured below may have been Fort Carmer. It was the original portion of a frame farmhouse that was attached to it for many years. (Above, courtesy of the National Park Service; below, author's collection.)

Col. Abraham VanCampen came to the Minisink in 1725 and purchased a large tract of land in Pahaquarry. VanCampen was a prominent figure in early New Jersey history, actively defending the frontier in the Native American wars of 1755. Sometime soon after he acquired the land, he built a stone house. A 20-foot square blockhouse was erected somewhere near the VanCampen house in 1756 to assist settlers on both sides of the river. Settlers in Pennsylvania had built a stockade around the Depui house, as the Native Americans were attacking settlements in Pennsylvania. An attack in January 1756 was cut short by extra men arriving from "the fort at VanCampen's" in Pahaquarry. The VanCampen house still stands today and is a private residence. The original stones have been covered in stucco, and dormers have been added along with other modifications. All traces of the old fort have long since disappeared. It was VanCampen's nephew Isaac who built the VanCampen Inn, located farther north in Walpack. (Courtesy of Rob Socha.)

The home of Isaac VanCampen served as a yaugh house during isolated Native American attacks, the French and Indian War, and the American Revolution. Fort Johns, also called headquarters and locally known as Fort Shapanack, was said to be located on the hill behind the VanCampen Inn, where the 1700s home of John Rosenkrans once stood. Rosenkrans's house was probably part of the fort, which is how it got the name Fort Johns. Archaeological evidence verified the existence of a stockade, but further digs did not uncover any more clues, leading some to theorize that the VanCampen house may have actually been the fort. The Army Corps of Engineers demolished the house on the hill and all outbuildings a year before the dig, so any other evidence of the fort was most likely obliterated. (Courtesy of the National Park Service.)

Fort Nominack (sometimes spelled Nomonack or Nomanock) is shown here in a photograph taken sometime in the 1930s. Conflicting reports often confuse Fort Nominack, so named because of its proximity to Nominack Island in the Delaware River, with the Westbrook fort associated with the Westbrook Bell House. The house fell to ruins not long after the photograph above was taken and was rapidly overgrown with vegetation. The site is nearly undetectable today. (Courtesy of the National Park Service.)

In 1756, there were probably about 400 Europeans living in the Minisink region of New Jersey. Of these, about a dozen were clustered near Walpack Bend and another dozen near Minisink Island in Montague. The rest were scattered along the river and in the valley. In the Montague area, very close to the Westbrook house (above), stood a stone building known as the Minisink fort or the Westbrook fort. Few records remain about the fort, but an archaeological survey confirmed this site as one of the minor military posts built in 1758. The fort is also mentioned in historical accounts of the Westbrook Bell House, which has a hidden passageway in the basement accessible only through a trapdoor in the living quarters. The passageway reportedly led to the deep ravine next to the house. During a raid, occupants left the house through the passageway and followed the ravine to the safety of the fort. (Courtesy of the Library of Congress, Prints and Photographs Division.)

Four

FROM SETTLEMENT TO COMMUNITY

In 1713, the Minisink patent granted permission for land along the Delaware River to be settled. Settlers seeking a new life left Esopus (Kingston, New York) and traveled south on the "good road to Esopus" to the "Menissinck."

Organized villages began appearing in the upper Delaware River valley in the beginning of the 1800s, though settlers had been in the valley for more than 100 years. Villages usually developed around a general store, a blacksmith shop, a gristmill, and a sawmill, which provided the basic services necessary for a community. With these businesses in place, churches, schools, a tavern or two, and homesteads soon followed.

Agriculture remained the focus throughout most of the 1800s. By the early 1900s, as methods of transportation improved, an interest in recreation began to replace a declining farming industry. The Delaware Water Gap became an especially popular location for summer resorts, and the towns north of the water gap prospered from the tourists passing through on their way south. Boardinghouses and hotels could be found in almost every community along the river in both Pennsylvania and New Jersey.

The northernmost village on the New Jersey side of the river was Millville, named for the gristmills and sawmills that were built there in the 1750s. Millville was finished as a village by 1872, but about a mile south, the village of Montague, or Brick House, was growing. Bevans, Walpack Center, Flatbrookville, Millbrook, Dunnfield, and Browning were the major villages in New Jersey.

In Pennsylvania, the northernmost village was Milford, established around 1793. Although Milford is across the bridge from Montague, it lies just outside the Delaware Water Gap National Recreation Area (DWGNRA). Dingmans Ferry, Bushkill, Maple Grove, and Dutotsburg-Delaware Water Gap were the major settlements on the Pennsylvania side of the river.

The advent of the automobile both doomed rural villages from rapid growth and saved them from urbanization. As families with cars traveled to larger cities to shop and trucks bypassed rural villages to deliver goods to urban communities, rural villages were spared the rush of progress, retaining much of their rural character well into the 1970s.

Religion was an important part of any community, and it usually did not take long before some type of church was constructed. The first churches were organized by ethnic groups. Since the Dutch were the first settlers in the upper Delaware River valley, most of the earliest churches were Dutch Reformed. As the Germans, the English, and the Scottish began to settle the valley, churches of other religious orientations appeared. The Minisink Dutch Reformed Church in Montague was organized in 1737, the same year the infamous Walking Purchase was taking place across the river in Pennsylvania. The church in this photograph predates 1888. It was replaced by a new building in 1899. (Courtesy of the Montague Association for Restoration and Community History.)

In 1776, Roger Clark built a brick house near the Delaware River in Montague. The building was constructed of odd-shaped bricks, fired in a local brick kiln. Called simply the Brick House, the building was an early stagecoach stop and hotel, which attracted enough people that a bustling community was established by 1881. A store, two blacksmith shops, a wheelwright shop, two churches, a one-room school, and a post office in the Brick House came to be known collectively as Brick House, or the village of Montague. Over the years, Brick House underwent many renovations to accommodate more guests. In 1953, Brick House was razed to make way for the approach to the new Milford-Montague toll bridge. (Courtesy of the Montague Association for Restoration and Community History.)

The town of Montague could never boast a booming population. In 1850, the population of Montague was 1,010, but by 1920, it had dropped to 534. Four one-room schools with small classes were still in use until 1953. In 1955, a new school started with only three classrooms. In the following years, only six additions followed; the last was in 1997. (Courtesy of the Montague Association for Restoration and Community History.)

The first of the Hornbeck family to settle in the Minisink area was Evert Hornbeck, born in 1698. It is uncertain whether his father came from Flanders (Belgium) or from the Dutch Republic (Netherlands), but his coming to America started a long line of Hornbecks in Montague. Probably the most well known of the Hornbeck family was George Hornbeck, born in 1830. The Hornbecks prospered from many business and farming deals, and George and his brothers came to own adjoining farms, which amounted to most of the land on the south side of Montague and around the Milford-Montague bridge. George died in 1902 after moving to Port Jervis. His younger brother continued to prosper by meeting the demands for fresh butter, dairy, and produce in the city and purchased George's Neldon farm a year after his brother's death. (Courtesy of the Montague Association for Restoration and Community History.)

The Grange (officially known as the Order of Patrons of Husbandry) was organized in 1867 by Oliver Hudson Kelley, a Minnesota farmer and activist. He believed that farmers, because of their independent and scattered nature, should have a national organization to represent them, much the same as unions were beginning to represent industrial workers. The local Grange chapter in Montague was often the focal point for community social events so important to rural residents. The Grange hosted educational events, dances, potlucks, town meetings, political rallies, and events for the local one-room schools, which did not have the facilities for school dances and other functions. The Montague Grange building was built over a period of years, beginning in 1905. (Courtesy of the Montague Association for Restoration and Community History.)

On a nice day sometime in 1900, nearly the whole town turned out for a clambake and picnic at the Montague Grange hall. Clambakes were usually held in the late summer, when the corn was ripe. What is a country clambake without fresh corn on the cob? (Courtesy of Patte Haggerty Frato.)

A community gathering was never complete without a pie-eating contest. Local farmers and residents celebrated holidays and the bounties of a good growing season with festivities held at the local Grange, the church hall, or sometimes in someone's big barn. These volunteers are competing in a pie-eating contest at the Grange hall in Montague. (Courtesy of the Montague Association for Restoration and Community History.)

In 1780, Peter Van Ness bought the land where the craft village of Peters Valley is now located. At one time, the village was called Hensfoot Corners, because the four roads that intersect there form a pattern not unlike a chicken's foot. Around 1880, the name changed to Bevans, in honor of the village postmaster, and is the name still preferred by some of the locals. The former Bevans general store now houses the craft store and gallery for the Peters Valley Crafts Education Center, which operates the craft village by special arrangement with the park service. The roofline and two chimneys of the c. 1855 Greek Revival house, which sits on a hill behind the store, can be seen in the photograph above. The Greek Revival building houses craft workshop participants. (Courtesy of Patte Haggerty Frato.)

Ferncliff House, Bevans, N. J.
(Wm. H. Titman, Prop.)

Across the road from the Bevans general store was Ferncliff House, which served as a hotel and tavern. Like most rural towns, Bevans underwent a population decline in the early 1900s, until tourists passing through the area discovered the village. By 1950, the population had again declined. Bevans became part of the DWGNRA in the early 1960s and shortly after was renamed Peters Valley, destined to become an art and craft center. Ferncliff House is still standing, although the large addition on the rear shown in this photograph (above) has been demolished. (Courtesy of Patte Haggerty Frato.)

The Post Office, Wallpack Center, N. J.

Isaac and Jasper Rundle opened a general store in 1850 to provide goods and services to the surrounding farms. By 1872, a blacksmith shop, a post office, a Methodist church, several residences, and a schoolhouse formed the village of Walpack (also Wallpack) Center. Although a quiet country village, Walpack was not without some notoriety. The race scene in the movie *These Thirty Years*, pitting horse and wagon against a new Ford car, was filmed in front of the Walpack general store around 1933. Walpack Center survived the horse-drawn carriage era and the new era of automobiles with its rural character intact. (Courtesy of Patte Haggerty Frato.)

MAIN ST., WALLPACK CENTER, N. J.

A card written and posted from "Cousin Anna" in Walpack in 1909 says, "It snowed all morning and now it is raining. We have only two views of Walpack. But I think there will be more taken before long. This is the store & on the stoop is Mrs. Roe & somebody I do not know. Mr. Roe stands out in front. These are the people who own the store." The people who owned the store at that time were Mr. and Mrs. E. S. Rosenkrans. The card was mailed to Anna's cousin Barbara McKeeby in Bevans. The first two buildings on the right side of the street, the Rosenkrans house and store, were next to the post office. Although the post office is no longer in use, the Rosenkrans house is now operated as a museum by the Walpack Historical Society through special arrangement with the park service. (Courtesy of Patte Haggerty Frato.)

Flatbrookville was a bit more prosperous than neighboring early villages because it was located on a major road and close to Decker's Ferry. The first gristmill was built on the Flatbrook around 1760. A sawmill was built before 1776. Flatbrookville did not come together as a village until the first general store and blacksmith shop were built in 1818. By 1844, there were about 20 homes, and by 1872, there were two blacksmith shops, a wheelwright shop, three general stores, a gristmill, a sawmill, a cooper shop, the Dutch Reformed church, and four mail routes through the village. A school (left), shown on the cover of a handmade cardboard book, opened in 1872. Flatbrookville began to decline in the early 1900s. Most of the village has been demolished; only two houses remain standing today. (Above, courtesy of Patte Haggerty Frato; left, courtesy of the National Park Service.)

Abram Garris built a gristmill in 1832 on VanCampens Brook that became the starting point for the village of Millbrook. The mill was more convenient for farmers who previously had to cross the river to Pennsylvania to process their grains. A Methodist church was built in 1839, and by 1840, a general store and blacksmith shop joined the community. Millbrook was a close-knit community, as traveling over the mountain to Flatbrookville was a difficult journey. Today Millbrook is a historical village, although only six buildings are original and the village does not authentically replicate the early linear village Millbrook once was. Other buildings in Millbrook have been relocated from elsewhere in the valley, most in preparation for the Tocks reservoir. (Courtesy of the National Park Service.)

The village of Dunnfield, located very close to the Delaware Water Gap, was a slate quarry company town. The slate company, owned in 1840 by Isaac Wycoff, employed 25 men to manufacture school slate. In 1860, Wycoff sold the company to the Delaware Water Gap Slate Company. The new company began quarrying slate in a nearby location, which spawned another company town called Browning, or Browntown. The photograph at left, taken at the slate factory in 1910, shows resident Alice Ace. Browning was abandoned in 1915 when the Delaware Water Gap Slate Company closed. In 1882, the New York, Susquehanna and Western Railroad built a depot for passengers and freight. Passengers traveled to and from the water gap resorts, and much of the freight included the slate produced in Dunnfield. Although the villages of Dunnfield and Browning ceased to exist when the slate company closed, the railroad continued to serve the tourist trade until the 1940s. (Courtesy of the National Park Service.)

Dingmans Ferry was first settled in 1735 by Andrew Dingman, who chose to build a sawmill, gristmill, and, later, a ferry service on Dingmans Creek, calling the place Dingmans Choice. Dingman's grandson Daniel constructed a hotel in 1812 and a school called Dingmans Academy in 1813. By 1820, Dingmans Choice had grown into a bustling village, spread in a line along the road. In 1836, a bridge replaced the ferry, and by the 1860s, the town had evolved into a tourist and summer vacation resort area with 10 hotels. The name changed to Dingmans Ferry in 1868 and continued to prosper when other area towns were in various stages of decline. In the 1970s, the Army Corps of Engineers removed all the structures in Dingmans Ferry except the church and the bridge, which continues operation as a privately owned toll bridge. (Courtesy of the National Park Service.)

In the early 1900s, baseball was the all-American sport, even in a small country town like Dingmans Ferry. The Dingmans baseball team is pictured here in 1904. Its biggest rivals were Bushkill, which was just south, and probably Milford, which was about the same distance to the north. By this time, Dingmans Ferry was attracting part of the tourist trade. Sometime around 1903, a troupe of Russians and their dancing bears visited the Delaware House, one of the larger hotels in Dingmans Ferry. (Courtesy of the National Park Service.)

Fort Hynshaw was among the first structures in Bushkill, erected on Bushkill Creek to protect the local settlers during the French and Indian War. A gristmill and tavern were already here, built in 1750. Another mill was built by Henry Peters in the early 1800s, and a tannery was added to the string of buildings in 1812. A blacksmith shop (above), a wagon shop, and a general store were added by 1824. Bushkill is another rural town that survived by catering to the tourist trade. By the 1880s, there were several boardinghouses and hotels whose businesses were given a boost in 1901 with the establishment of the Delaware Valley Railroad. The Peters House (below) was one of the largest boardinghouses and survived into the 20th century. (Courtesy of the National Park Service.)

During the tourist years, the ground floor of the Bushkill mill was used as a small local restaurant. The first level of the Bushkill mill was filled with artifacts and goods that reflected an earlier and simpler way of life. For a brief time, the ground level of the mill was used as a restaurant. Patrons at the mill could enjoy a meal surrounded by the ambiance of the old mill. Peters Mill burned to the ground in 1980; only the stone foundation remains. (Courtesy of the Library of Congress, Prints and Photographs Division.)

Most of the late-19th-century schools in Pennsylvania shared the same type of construction and were still one-room buildings. The River School (above) near Shawnee on Delaware was built of stone in 1888 but featured a roof-framing system that included wood- and iron-truss members. The Union School (below), shown here in 1879, is very similar to the River School. (Courtesy of the National Park Service.)

North Water Gap Mill, North Water Gap, Pa.

Dutotsburg, which later became Delaware Water Gap, and the area called North Water Gap in Pennsylvania, also had a large gristmill complex. This town was rather prosperous during the late 1800s and early 1900s, being located very close to the Delaware Water Gap itself. (Courtesy of Patte Haggerty Frato.)

Five

AGRICULTURE AND INDUSTRY

Agriculture in the upper Delaware River valley is one of the hallmarks from the past that survived into the present day, albeit under very different conditions. The Native Americans supplemented hunting game with growing corn, beans, and squash on the river flatlands, practiced crop rotation, and burned fields to keep vegetation from overgrowing. Learning from the Lenapes, the first settlers to arrive in the valley laid claim to the flat, fertile river bottomlands in both New Jersey and Pennsylvania. Corn is the major crop planted now by farmers who cultivate the fields under special agreements with the National Park Service. Today former farm fields that are not cultivated are mowed regularly to prevent overgrowth, thus preserving the open fields that were once part of the cultural landscape.

The design of the first houses was based on the ethnic origin of the settlers, but many reflected the ingenuity and resourcefulness of these early settlers. The first homes were probably one- or two-room log cabins. The Dutch first built a sawed log structure on a stone foundation, but they much preferred and later constructed homes from limestone and fieldstone. Until a barn could be built, farmers constructed a type of open shed with a thatched roof to shelter their animals. The barn was built as soon as the house was habitable. Other outbuildings on a farm, which generally averaged about 300 acres, included a springhouse, a smokehouse, an icehouse, small sheds to house poultry and hogs, and granaries. Wagon sheds, woodsheds, corncribs, and silos came later.

Farming settlers were basically self-sufficient. Crops were planted not only to feed the farmer's family but also to feed the livestock. Women planted and tended their own vegetable gardens, which usually were not far from the kitchen.

Early industries often grew from the needs of the first settlers. Slate was quarried for roofing and school slates, gristmills were needed to grind harvested grains, lumber was needed for building, and rafts and boats were needed to transport goods on the river. Mining and slate quarry industries also attracted some of the first settlers into the upper Delaware River valley.

The first industry in the upper Delaware River valley was probably copper mining at Pahaquarry, a few miles north of the Delaware Water Gap in New Jersey. Although never very prosperous, the mines were worked on and off until the 1920s. There is also a story about one individual living alone in a hut near the Pahaquarry mines who spent the summer mining copper and silver from caves deep in the mountain. He coined illegal but profitable money from the metals he collected and made enough to live in a palatial house in some remote city with his family during the winter. Who he was is uncertain, and the truth of the story is unknown, but perhaps counterfeiting was at least one enterprising industry in the Delaware Water Gap. Although a 1700s coin was recovered in the upper Delaware River valley, it was of legitimate origin. (Courtesy of the National Park Service.)

One of the finest examples of a preindustrial 18th-century farm in the Delaware River valley was the Walter Kautz farm on River Road in Pennsylvania. The house was erected on the former site of the log Smithfield Dutch Reformed Church and was built sometime between 1825 and 1844. The farm was one that prospered through the years, as evidenced by a growing collection of outbuildings. (Courtesy of the National Park Service.)

The Kautz farm, with the exception of the years 1889 to 1891, remained in the Kautz family until it was sold to the federal government in 1968. The photograph was taken around 1905. The log watering trough in the lower right corner of the photograph was kept filled to offer fresh water to passing teams of horses and drivers. (Courtesy of the National Park Service.)

The buildings and layout of the farm were evidence of the farm's success through the years. Pictured from left to right are the corncrib–wagon shed, icehouse, washhouse-woodshed, house, and barn. The beams for the barn were hand-hewed by Jim Treible, the last of the flatboat builders. Barns were the first structures to be built after the house, and other outbuildings were then added as needed. (Courtesy of the Library of Congress, Prints and Photographs Division.)

One of the most unique structures on the Kautz farm was the corncrib–wagon shed combination building, which reflected the ingenuity of conserving space and building materials by combining two functions into one structure. It was built partially into a bank, with room for produce and corn storage on the bottom floor. There were no floorboards on the north wall of the second level, which allowed the corncrib to be filled from above. (Courtesy of the National Park Service.)

The slatted walls of the corncrib allowed for ventilation, while five hatches at various heights and a door at the bottom of the stairs allowed access to the corn. Wagons were stored on the second floor or on the bottom floor, which was open at both ends. (Courtesy of the Library of Congress, Prints and Photographs Division.)

Another combination building was the washhouse and woodshed, adjacent to the main house. The upper level served as a workshop, and the ground floor was half washroom, half wood storage. Most farms in the Delaware River valley had all these outbuildings but not combined into one structure. (Courtesy of the National Park Service.)

The barn was the first building to be constructed after the family secured a safe place to live. While the barn was under construction, animals were sheltered by a poled run-in shed with a thatched roof. The Dutch barn, first described by Peter Kalm in 1748, was a large building with a shingle or gable roof and doors at the gable ends, which allowed a wagon to be pulled through the structure. Animals were stabled on either side. A threshing floor was in the middle, and above it was a loft for unthreshed grain and straw. The Dutch barn at the Isaac VanCampen Inn (above) was a classic example of this style barn. It was destroyed by an arsonist in 1972. A similar Dutch barn survives today on the Westbrook Bell and Black Minisink farm property in Sandyston Township. Since the photograph below was taken, the barn has been stabilized and resided by the National Park Service. (Courtesy of the National Park Service.)

During the winter, ice was seldom a shortage on the Delaware River. In fact, it could back up in huge chunks, called an ice jam, resulting in some flooding and crop damage when the river thawed in the spring. One building common to most homesteads was the icehouse, usually constructed of stone and fairly small in size. Proper drainage and a sufficient amount of ice in storage were vital to the successful functioning of an icehouse. Ice was stored either on a bed of gravel or on an elevated timber floor and packed in straw or sawdust. Two-room icehouses were designed to also provide cool food storage. (Courtesy of the National Park Service.)

Ice was harvested from the river, usually in January. Ice cutting was difficult and dangerous work and required many hands to efficiently bring the cut blocks back to the icehouse. Snow had to first be cleared from the river. Once the ice was exposed, axes were used to punch holes in it to create a starting point from which blocks could be cut. Ropes and chains were always kept nearby in case people or horses fell through. At other times, the river provided floating chunks of ice that could be harvested. Those living too far from the river harvested ice in a similar manner from the farm pond. (Courtesy of the National Park Service.)

The original section of the DeWitt farmhouse was built in 1798 on the main road from Daniel Decker's ferry across the river at Walpack Bend. John DeWitt came to the area in the early 1770s, and by 1790, he had acquired 300 acres of land and two dwellings for $2,100, and another 69-acre parcel and one dwelling for $275. This farmhouse was lit by kerosene lamps until 1948, and in 1959, a bath and shower were installed. (Courtesy of the National Park Service.)

Women took care of the house, milked cows, fed farm animals, kept the kitchen garden, cleaned, cooked, sewed the clothing after spinning the yarn and making the cloth, made small repairs, made soap, healing ointments, and salves, and taught these skills to their daughters—and all while wearing long, cumbersome dresses. (Courtesy of the National Park Service.)

Between grain harvests, farmers cut fields of native grass to use for hay. Cutting hay was often a group effort, as there was no machinery to do the job. Hay was cut by hand using sickles or scythes. After it dried, the hay was raked into piles for pick up or left piled in the field and fenced off to prevent the animals from eating the stacks. (Courtesy of the Montague Association for Restoration and Community History.)

Some farmers loaded hay onto wagons and stored it in hayracks or, later, in barn lofts to keep it dry. Most farmers allowed their animals free grazing during the summer, feeding stored hay, corn, straw, and oats during the winter. In the early days, oxen were preferred for farmwork, but in later years, draft horses began to outnumber oxen. (Author's collection.)

From his stone house on the Old Mine Road, Alonzo Depue provided a unique service in Sandyston Township. Depue lived in the house and ran the farm, and he served as a U.S. weather observer from 1914 to 1962. He was also the township treasurer for 33 years, a member of the board of education for 28 years, and a teacher for 14 years. The Depue house, built around 1810, is unusual in that it has been altered very little even though it has had many owners and is known locally as "that house with three chimneys." The house has been vacant since it was acquired by the Army Corps of Engineers. Once a thriving farm with several outbuildings, only the house remains today, with a historical monument to Depue on the front lawn. (Courtesy of the National Park Service.)

In its heyday, the Depue farm was a working dairy farm, with a large barn and several outbuildings across the road from the house. The house had a wooden addition at the rear that was built sometime before 1900, but this no longer stands. A beehive oven on the end wall is still visible from the outside of the house today. (Courtesy of the National Park Service.)

When this photograph was taken, probably in the late 1890s, the Depue family gathered in front of the house for a picture. A good horse, a good carriage, a fine house, and a prosperous farm were more than most folks could hope for. It is no wonder they brought out their best horses and fine carriage for this photograph. (Courtesy of the National Park Service.)

As farms in the valley prospered, the need for mills and other industries soon surfaced. The Bushkill mill was built in 1840 and still had the original gristmill machinery intact, including wooden shafts, cogs, gears, and millstones, when the government acquired the property in the 1960s. According to the deeds, there was also a tavern house and a sawmill at the site. The mill remained in operation until 1928. Small local mills fell by the wayside as the center of grain production moved to the Midwest, and improvements in transportation and shipping allowed for a larger distribution from these areas. (Courtesy of the Library of Congress, Prints and Photographs Division.)

Haney's Mill, located on the Flatbrook between Walpack Center and Flatbrookville, was a combination sawmill, cider mill, and gristmill. The picturesque Haney's Mill appeared in the May 1933 issue of *National Geographic*. There was also a limekiln and two or three houses on the property, all of which are now gone except for scattered remains of the stone foundation and a concrete wing dam bearing the inscription, "J. Haney, 1926," for Jake Haney, the last mill operator. (Courtesy of Patte Haggerty Frato.)

A narrow bridge over the Flatbrook, built in 1891 and appropriately called the Haney's Mill bridge, allowed visitors to cross the Flatbrook and visit Haney's Mill. In the early days, they arrived on foot, on horseback, or in horse-drawn carriages. (Courtesy of Patte Haggerty Frato.)

In 1915, one of the first automobiles in Walpack crossed the bridge to Haney's Mill. The car belonged to Haney, the mill operator, and was immortalized in a 1915 postcard. (Courtesy of Patte Haggerty Frato.)

By the mid-1700s, logging was a major industry in the Delaware River valley. Several hundred logs could be lashed together and floated downriver as rafts, all the way to Easton and Philadelphia. When the railroads came, railroad ties became a new market, and some rafts were stopped at the water gap and transported elsewhere by the railroad. (Courtesy of the Montague Association for Restoration and Community History.)

It is believed that Daniel Skinner sent the first log raft down the Delaware River in 1764. That raft consisted of six 70-foot pine logs destined to become masts for sailing ships under construction in Philadelphia. It is recorded that, in 1829, more than 1,000 rafts and 50 million feet of lumber made their way down the river. The rafting industry peaked around 1850 and significantly declined thereafter, coming to a close at the dawn of the 20th century. (Courtesy of the National Park Service.)

Shad Fishermen Loading Their Half-Mile of Net (Value $1,500 For Another Haul, Delaware River, Philadelphia. Copyright 1905 by E. W. Kelley.

Like farming, fishing has survived along the Delaware since the first Paleo people inhabited the valley. Early settlers conducted fish drives by cutting enough brush to float downriver toward a prebuilt blockage. Fish driven ahead of the brush into the shallow water could easily be caught. Another method utilized nets woven together on the barn floor and suspended between boats. The net was allowed to drift with the current into a semicircle and then was hauled ashore. The American shad, the largest of the herring family in North America, return to the Delaware River to spawn each spring. In 1905, when this photograph was taken, a half-mile shad net yielded $1,500 worth of fish. (Courtesy of the National Park Service.)

The Pahaquarry copper mines evolved into a large mining community by the early 1900s. The owners of the mine at that time spent a lot of money and effort to build a large mining facility, which did not pay off. By 1910, the complex included an office, a blacksmith shop, a tipple mill barn, an icehouse, and a boardinghouse for the miners. The company remained in debt, and the complex was sold at a sheriff's sale in 1918. In 1925, the Trenton Council of Boy Scouts purchased the property to use the land. Several subsequent attempts were made to mine the copper, but it was never deemed worthwhile. For a time during the late 1800s and into the early 1900s, the mines were somewhat of a tourist attraction, being within an easy ride from the resort hotels in the Delaware Water Gap. (Courtesy of the National Park Service.)

Henry Shoemaker arrived in Pahaquarry in 1790 and built a two-and-a-half-story rubble stone house somewhere around 1795. When he died, the building went first to his eldest daughter and then to her brother Samuel Shoemaker. Samuel operated the Union Hotel, a lodging place for raftsmen on the river. The post office was also located here, with Samuel serving as the postmaster. He also ran a ferry from this location. The Union Hotel was extensively remodeled in 1908 and 1947 and was a tavern in the late 1960s when acquired by the Army Corps of Engineers. Today it is better known as the Copper Mine Inn due to its proximity to the old Pahaquarry copper mine sites. The building is vacant but still standing. (Courtesy of the Library of Congress, Prints and Photographs Division.)

The slate quarries that once operated in the Delaware River valley were among the first commercial enterprises in the country, beginning as early as 1734. The first quarries were located near the river, which provided a means of transportation for materials and supplies. The Delaware Water Gap Slate Company's landholdings along the Delaware River in Warren County formed part of the village of Browning, or Browntown. The quarry was in operation from 1870 to 1904. Browning slate workers lived in company housing. The village included a factory for manufacturing roof and school slate, a blacksmith shop, a company store, offices, and the superintendent's house. (Courtesy of the National Park Service.)

Six

BOATS, TRAINS, AND AUTOMOBILES

Prior to the advent of the automobile and subsequent improvement of roadways, getting around in the upper Delaware River valley was difficult at best. Most roads were not much more than Native American trails, only two or three feet wide. The landscape was often treacherous. When the Europeans arrived, they used these trails, later widening them to accommodate wagons and carriages.

The Dutch had constructed a wagon road from Esopus (Kingston, New York) to their settlement at Machackemack (present-day Port Jervis), which later extended about six miles south in New Jersey. This was an original segment of the Old Mine Road, supposedly built by the Dutch to transport copper ore from the mines in Pahaquarra to Esopus as early as 1650. While mention of both the copper mines and the road appear in early writings, historians now disagree whether the road existed as early as once thought. It is reasonable to assume that a road existed from the northern sections of New Jersey to Pahaquarra by the 1750s, as building the line of aforementioned forts during the French and Indian War would have necessitated having a road. In addition, mining was taking place in Pahaquarra and a means of transporting the ore was required.

Conditions were similar in Pennsylvania. The Minisink Trail was the major path, entering the upper Delaware River valley at the water gap. Native American trails, wagon roads, and River Road became the major land routes in Pennsylvania.

Of course, the Delaware River was both a barrier to land travel and an alternative means of transportation. In certain locations, crossing the river could be achieved during times of low water but could be hazardous in high water or during the winter. Durham boats, such as the type George Washington used to cross the Delaware River during the American Revolution, were used on the river to transport supplies. They preceded the flat-bottomed ferryboats that appeared shortly after the first settlers. Ferry crossings were available at almost every major settlement. Steamboats followed, but the real boon to travel in the upper Delaware River valley arrived with the railroad in 1847.

The improvements in land and river transportation increased trade and made life easier for the folks in the valley.

Early roads in the upper Delaware River valley were sometimes treacherous. Heavy rains created mountain waterfalls capable of washing out a road in minutes. Ruts created by wagon wheels dried solid and deep. In good weather, travelers had to contend with dust, dirt, rocks, and an inevitable bumpy ride. This photograph was taken on the Old Mine Road between Walpack Center and Flatbrookville. (Courtesy of Patte Haggerty Frato.)

Early land travel was by foot, horseback, or horse and carriage. By the late 1790s, several county commissioners and township officials were taking measures to improve the roads. Usually these measures included ordering residents to maintain the road in their area as a public road. By 1801, some private groups began maintaining roads and charging tolls to use them. (Courtesy of the National Park Service.)

Stagecoach lines connected the major towns with one another. The Brick House, site of the village of Montague, was a regular stop for the New York to Oswego line, as well as the old stage from Deckertown (present-day Sussex) to Jersey City. (Courtesy of the Montague Association for Restoration and Community History.)

Horses were not only used for personal transportation and stagecoaches but also were vital to many of the local business and services, such as the J. P. Nearpass milk wagon that delivered milk and dairy to folks in Montague. (Courtesy of the Montague Association for Restoration and Community History.)

The Durham boat was designed by Robert Durham specifically to transport cargo on the Delaware River. The boats were large flat-bottomed boats measuring 60 feet long by 8 feet wide by 42 inches deep, with high vertical sides. The Durham boat could carry a load of 17 tons going downstream and 2 tons when traveling upstream. A crew of three men used 12- to 18-foot-long poles for steering while going downstream. Traveling upstream required more work, as the crew had to use the poles to push the boats while walking back and forth on walking boards built into the sides. Canal boats later joined the Durham boats in transporting goods on the river. (Courtesy of the National Park Service.)

The Delaware River is not a particularly wide river, and most of it is fairly calm. It is possible to stand on one shore and clearly see the activities on the opposite shore. Colonial or state governments issued charters under which the first ferryboats were permitted to operate. (Courtesy of the National Park Service.)

Ferryboats differed in size but were all basically flat-bottom boats with squared ends. They were wide enough to accommodate horses and a large wagon. In shallow, calm water, ferries were propelled or guided by long poles, much like their Durham boat predecessors, and by rope cables at each end secured on the shore. (Courtesy of the National Park Service.)

Decker's Ferry began service between 1744 and 1756 at Walpack Bend, running across the river to Smithfield Township on the Pennsylvania shore. Col. Philip Van Cortland's army used Decker's Ferry to cross the river in 1779 on its way to join Maj. Gen. John Sullivan in Pennsylvania. Decker's Ferry was sold to Eugene Rosenkrans in 1882, who ran it until 1898. Rosenkrans's son moved it upriver and made the crossing to Stroudsburg. (Courtesy of the National Park Service.)

Henry Shoemaker's ferry started its service in 1792. It was operated by his son for many years and then sold to several owners before being discontinued in the early 1920s. Dimmick's Ferry, just upstream from Shoemaker's, started around 1820. It was sold to William Fisher and for some time operated as Fisher's Ferry, but it was purchased by Michael Dimmick in 1881, and the ferry resumed the Dimmick name. (Courtesy of the National Park Service.)

Dimmick's Ferry was operated by two steel cables. An overhead cable attached to one shoreline allowed the ferry to operate in high water. When the water was low, a cable lying on the bottom of the river was used to pull the ferry across. Dimmick's Ferry ceased operation in 1927. (Courtesy of the National Park Service.)

Meyers Ferry operated at the Delaware Water Gap. It also was propelled by a high-water cable suspended above the river, visible in this early-1900s photograph. (Courtesy of the National Park Service.)

In 1860, the first steamboat was built for travel on the Delaware River. On its maiden voyage, while carrying several politicians and dignitaries, the boilers on the *Alfred Thomas* were pushed beyond their limits, and the boat exploded, killing 13 passengers. In 1879, Luke Brodhead introduced the *Kittatinny*, a 50-passenger steamboat, shown here on the river behind the rowboats. The *Kittatinny* ran moonlight cruises on the Delaware River for just 25¢ per passenger. (Courtesy of the National Park Service.)

Beautiful View of Delaware Water Gap from Trolley.

Railroads shared track with trolleys running from Stroudsburg to Portland, Pennsylvania. The Philadelphia and Western Railway Company did not grant the trolleys use of its tracks at Portland, so passengers had to get off one trolley, collect their baggage, and cross the tracks to board another trolley to get to the Delaware Water Gap. By 1926, trolley service to the Delaware Water Gap was cancelled. (Courtesy of the National Park Service.)

One of the most important railroad connections in the Delaware Water Gap happened on the Pennsylvania side of the river in 1856 when the Delaware, Lackawanna and Western Railroad completed track from the Delaware Water Gap to New York City, which had a huge impact on the tourist trade in the upper Delaware River valley. (Courtesy of the Library of Congress, Prints and Photographs Division.)

In the early years of train travel, a coal-powered steam train was a dirty ride, and passengers could look forward to reaching their destination covered with black soot. Trains powered by clean-burning anthracite coal were the exception. Since the Delaware, Lackawanna and Western Railroad owned several anthracite mines in Pennsylvania, it could boast a clean ride. Its advertising department took advantage of that fact and invented a fictional character named Phoebe Snow, a young New York socialite. Snow was a frequent passenger on the train and always dressed in white to prove to passengers that they would remain clean and soot-free while traveling on a Lackawanna. Snow's career ended with the start of World War II, when the need for anthracite coal for the war effort prohibited its use on trains. Snow had become such a popular mascot for the train that in 1949, the Lackawanna named a new streamlined passenger train the *Phoebe Snow*. (Courtesy of the National Park Service.)

Although boasting a clean train ride, anthracite companies were often the scene of child labor. Breaker boys were used to pick slate from Pennsylvania anthracite coal companies in the early 1900s until A. Langerfeld introduced a machine for picking coal in 1913. The new automated process eliminated the use of breaker boys, and the new machine was much more accurate. (Courtesy of the Library of Congress, Prints and Photographs Division.)

RATES OF TOLL ONE WAY

4 WHEEL CARRIAGE, 4 HORSES	50 CTS.
4 " " 2 "	25 "
WAGON, 2 HORSES, MULES OR OXEN	25 "
EACH ADDITIONAL HORSE MULE OR OX	5 "
CART 2 HORSES OR MULES	25 "
1 HORSE WAGON OR SLEIGH	20 "
MAN & HORSE	7 "
HORSE MULE OR JACK	5 "
COW OR OTHER CATTLE	3 "
20 SHEEP OR HOGS	20 "
LARGE AUTO TRUCK	40 "
AUTO TRUCK WITH TRAILER	50 "
7 PASSENGER CAR	30 "
5 " "	25 "
2 " "	20 "
2 SEATED MOTOR CYCLES	10 "
MOTOR & SIDE CAR	10 "
BICYCLE	5 "
TANDEM	5 "
FOOTMEN	2 "

The advent of the automobile did away with the ferryboats and eventually the railroads. The first toll bridge between Milford and Montague opened for business in 1826. An ice freshet dislodged the New Jersey span of the bridge in 1841 and beached it at Minisink Island. In 1846, this scenario was repeated. A replacement bridge was rapidly built, which collapsed a few years later. In 1869, a suspension bridge using John Roebling's design was built but was also swept away by a flood in 1888. The next bridge was an iron suspension bridge, and although very scary to cross by all local accounts, it survived until the current Milford-Montague toll bridge was built in 1953, just south of the former bridge site. The current bridge is higher and wider than its predecessors and has survived subsequent floods on the Delaware River, including the infamous flood of 1955. The toll today is 75¢ per car. (Courtesy of the Montague Association for Restoration and Community History.)

Seven

THE RESORT ERA

Life in the cities of New York and Philadelphia, in an era without modern facilities, air-conditioning, and other amenities of daily living that are now take for granted, was rather unpleasant in the heat and humidity of summer. Malaria and other diseases swept through populated areas. It is not surprising that the fresh air, cool breezes, and sparkling waters of the Delaware Water Gap beckoned and that resort hotels enjoyed a booming business well into the 1900s. By the end of the Civil War, the Delaware Water Gap was the second-largest inland resort, with Saratoga Springs ranking first.

Advertisements for the 40 or so hotels that once populated the Delaware Water Gap emphasized the clean air, the healthy atmosphere, and a completely mosquito-free region. Mountain springs and streams provided fresh water, and many of the hotels also maintained their own farms for meats and vegetables.

Unlike traveling today where a vacation translates into a week or two away from home, Victorian-era women and children spent the summer in the mountains while dad went to work in the cities and joined them on the weekend.

The earliest visitors came by horse-drawn wagons and the stagecoach, but by the mid-1800s, railroads and trolley cars made getting to the Delaware River much more convenient. The railroad brought an increase in the tourist trade, and an estimated one million people made their way to the water gap every summer. Towns everywhere in the Minisink prospered from the increased travel, and many home owners earned extra cash by opening their homes to tourists.

The largest and most lavish hotels were the Water Gap House and the Kittatinny House. Six boardinghouses were located about half a mile to three miles distant from the Kittatinny and Water Gap Houses, including Brainerd House, Lenape House, Glenwood House, River Farm House, Analoming House, and Highland Dale House, with others in nearby Stroudsburg. Most of the hotels were on the Pennsylvania side of the river, where natural steppes in the mountain were friendlier to construction.

The advent of the automobile brought both prosperity and the death knell for the resort industry. At first, families came by the carload, and motor touring the countryside was a popular pastime. As people became more mobile, however, the water gap was within a few hours' drive, and fewer people decided to stay for an extended period of time. The Depression years signaled the final downturn for the resort era.

As early as the 1820s, people began coming into the Delaware Water Gap region to enjoy the wild beauty of the mountains and swimming, fishing, and canoeing the river. Since there were no hotels, it did not take long for area residents to recognize the opportunity to make some extra money, and many of them rented out rooms for the summer to the tourists. People were

attracted to the clean, fresh air, lack of mosquitoes, and abundance of nature in the water gap. By the end of the Civil War, it was well known all along the East Coast as a popular vacation spot. (Courtesy of the Library of Congress, Prints and Photographs Division.)

In 1829, Antoine Dutot noticed the influx of people coming to vacation in the mountains. Ever the businessman, Dutot began construction of a hotel situated on the first geological step of Mount Minsi, but he soon ran out of money and sold the unfinished hotel to Samuel Snyder in 1832. Snyder finished the building, named it the Kittatinny House, and filled its 25-guest capacity the first season. (Courtesy of the Library of Congress, Prints and Photographs Division.)

The Kittatinny House was rented by William Brodhead in 1841. By 1851, Brodhead had purchased the hotel and increased its size over the next 15 years to its final capacity of 250 guests in 1860. (Courtesy of the Library of Congress, Prints and Photographs Division.)

Luke Willis Brodhead managed the Kittatinny House, and in 1867 and 1870, he published a small book called *The Delaware Water Gap: Its Scenery, Its Legends and Early History*, in which he describes areas around the gap as the "playgrounds of his boyhood, the rambles of his youth, and . . . the admiration of his manhood." Brodhead later went on to build the Water Gap House in 1872. All the many Brodhead brothers (below) were actively involved in the early tourist businesses of the Delaware Water Gap. (Courtesy of the National Park Service.)

The palatial, columned lobby of the Kittatinny House (above) was both elegant and country comfortable. Bright and airy, the lobby was impressive with its tall columns, high ceilings, fireplace, and wicker furnishings. This elegant country flavor was repeated in the sitting rooms (below), where guests could enjoy pleasant conversation. Many guests spent the days exploring the mountains, and in the evening, the fireplace mantel was frequently adorned with tumblers filled with colorful flowers and mosses. Men who went fishing brought their catch to the cook, who prepared a special meal for the fishermen. Hikers, botanists, and birdwatchers gathered in the lobby and sitting areas to exchange stories about the day's adventures and to make plans for the next outing. (Courtesy of the National Park Service.)

Many of the guests booked their stay for the whole summer. Women and children remained at the resorts while working husbands returned to the cities during the week, making the long journey back to the water gap on the weekends, at first by coach, trolley, and train and later by automobile. Wealthier families that were fortunate enough to take time off from business enjoyed a true extended vacation away from the stifling heat of the cities. (Courtesy of the Library of Congress, Prints and Photographs Division.)

The Kittatinny House was built on one of a series of geological steps or plateaus in the Pennsylvania mountains about 180 feet above the river. A mountain stream rushed through the huge kitchen and was used to cool perishable foods. The hotel veranda offered a commanding view of the river but only a partial view of the gap itself. The veranda was a favorite spot for guests to gather and socialize. On one rainy day in the 1870s, guests were enjoying an August rainstorm from the veranda when the sun broke through the clouds over the gap, and a brilliantly colored rainbow appeared, arching across the break in the mountains from shore to shore. The skies over the hotel remained leaden, with no sign of sunshine. Those observing the phenomenon thought the sight exceedingly beautiful and evidence enough that the gap was surely bewitched. (Courtesy of the National Park Service.)

In the late 19th century, guests paid from $3.50 to $4.50 per day or $10 to $21 per week to stay at the Kittatinny House, arriving by horse and carriage, trolley, railroad, and, later, automobiles. The hotel boasted electricity and all the amenities. The large electrified fountain in the courtyard of the Kittatinny House was a notable attraction and a favorite place for an after-dinner stroll around the grounds. (Courtesy of the National Park Service.)

A tallyho coach, a fast coach drawn by four horses, shuttled passengers between the train stations and the hotels. Stagecoaches, like the one photographed below in 1867, were the mode of transportation before the trains. With the advent of the railroads and the automobile, the use of stagecoaches gradually diminished as a mode of major transportation to the mountain resorts. Horse-drawn carriages were still used by the hotels to shuttle passengers to and from the hotel and the train and trolley stations. (Courtesy of the National Park Service.)

The coming of the railroad to the Delaware Water Gap area brought a huge influx of tourists every summer. The Delaware, Lackawanna and Western Railroad, formed from the merger of two smaller railroad companies, ran the first train from Scranton to the Delaware Water Gap in 1856. A train departing New York at 7:30 a.m. arrived at the water gap at 1:15 p.m. Crowds gathered early at the train stations. Passengers traveled in luxurious club cars and enjoyed the journey as part of their vacation. In 1895, a ticket from New York to the gap cost $2.55. (Courtesy of the Library of Congress, Prints and Photographs Division.)

Because of a series of level plateaus or steps on the sides of Mount Minsi, there was room for a large building like the Kittatinny House, as well as the railroad tracks and roadways around the hotel. One would not suspect such a level area when looking at the hotel from the river. There was plenty of room in front of the Kittatinny House for cars, carriages, and beautiful gardens, and if it were not for the view, one could easily forget that the hotel was built on the side of a mountain. (Courtesy of the National Park Service.)

In the mid-1800s, golf was a popular game in Europe and Scotland, but did not make an appearance in the United States until the late 1800s. In 1898, a chemist in Ohio invented a method of making golf balls by winding rubber thread under tension around a central core. Golf rapidly became a popular sport by the end of the 19th century, and by 1931, there were 238 public golf courses. The hotel resorts in the Delaware Water Gap wasted no time in providing guests with golf courses. The Water Gap House claimed to have one of the finest and most attractive links in the east within a three-minute walk of the hotel. In the photograph below, golfers enjoy the game at the eighth hole of the Caldena Golf Links in Pennsylvania. (Courtesy of the National Park Service.)

The Water Gap House was opened in 1872 by Luke Willis Brodhead. Piazzas on the first and second floors were 12 to 15 feet wide and 650 feet in length, providing guests with the finest view of the river. The Water Gap House was sold to new owner John Purdy Cope, who spent more than $100,000 in 1908 to completely rebuild the hotel. An advertisement in the June 14, 1908, *New York Times* told readers the Water Gap House had a "capacity 300. A mountain paradise; highest altitude, coolest location, always a breeze, no humidity . . . Commanding views for 30 miles in every direction of the grandest scenery east of the Rockies . . . entertaining refined, high-class patronage . . . telephone and telegraphs, Solariums and balconies on all floors. Steam heat, open log fireplaces. Electric lights. Hydraulic elevator. Most modern sanitary arrangements . . . Hotel supplied by own greenhouse and farm . . . Milk from own dairy of registered cows. Every outdoor sport and indoor amusement. Orchestra and frequent social functions. Private riding academy with high-class saddle horses and instructors; nine-hole golf links; garage and livery—all within the grounds. Coaches meet all trains." (Courtesy of the National Park Service.)

Pres. Theodore Roosevelt visited the Water Gap House on August 2, 1910. After his visit, he wrote, "I have never supposed that so lovely a resort was situated among the hills at so comparatively short distance." Just five years later, on the afternoon of November 11, 1915, workers preparing to close the hotel for the winter happened upon a fire in one of the guest rooms. Although the alarm was sounded and fire companies from several nearby towns responded, the entire hotel was leveled in just a few hours in a spectacular fire that could be seen for miles. The loss was estimated between $150,000 and $200,000. Days after the devastating fire, an announcement was made that a new bigger, better, fireproof hotel would be built on the site and would be open for the 1916 season, but the hotel was never built. (Courtesy of the National Park Service.)

Horseback riding and, in some cases, burro riding were a popular attraction in the Delaware Water Gap. Burros were calmer and more sure-footed than horses and were more reliable on mountain trails, sidesaddle or not. (Courtesy of the National Park Service.)

The game of billiards evolved from an outdoor game similar to croquet. Tables had low walls called banks because they resembled riverbanks. In the early 1800s, billiard tables were lit by candles, and by 1864, most of the better tables had slate beds. The billiard room at the Kittatinny House was roomy, had electricity, and probably smelled of cigar smoke. (Courtesy of the Library of Congress, Prints and Photographs Division.)

Guests of the mountain resorts were encouraged to view the majestic water gap from many different vantage points. In 1870, William Brodhead, owner of the Kittatinny House, wrote, "Taking a small boat, at the foot of the cliff on which the hotel is situated, and rowing down over the quiet waters, affords, perhaps, the most impressive view, such as you will ever remember with pleasure. You can better realize the height of the mountain, the width of the chasm, the serpentine course of the river, and the force required to produce the dislocation." Guests could take a small rowboat or canoe from the hotel's fleet and paddle their own way on the quiet river. Some of the boats were even equipped with chairs for the ladies. (Courtesy of the National Park Service.)

Short-story writer and entomologist Annie Trumball Slosson (1838–1926) was photographed in 1910 in front of the Water Gap House. Slosson epitomized the American local color movement that flourished after the Civil War and ended at the beginning of the 20th century. Her first work was *The China Hunter's Club* (1878), but her two most important volumes were *Seven Dreamers* (1890) and *Dumb Foxglove and Other Stories* (1898). (Courtesy of the National Park Service.)

Although most of the large hotels were located in the Delaware Water Gap, and the gap was definitely the center of attention, many of the smaller towns also benefited from the tourist industry. Nearly every town from the gap north to Montague had some type of hotel or guesthouse. These houses were more comparable to present-day bed-and-breakfasts, accommodating visitors and tourists for short-term or long-term stays in the valley. Most of the boardinghouses were private residences whose owners rented out the extra bedrooms. The Kerr boardinghouse (above) and the DeRemer House (at left) were two popular houses in Montague. (Courtesy of the Montague Association for Restoration and Community History.)

Eight

FLOOD, FEAR, AND FIASCO

Floods on the Delaware River are nothing new. People have an uncanny ability to establish homes on the banks of a river, only to scream foul when the river floods. Most floods are not that severe, but there are always exceptions. The flood of 1955 was the most exceptional of all, and even though most of the deaths attributed to it were on Brodhead Creek and not the Delaware River, the government saw an opportunity to get involved. The Tocks Island dam project was born.

Shortly after the dam was authorized in 1962, the Army Corps of Engineers began to quickly acquire properties in the Delaware River valley. In the following years, the government continued to acquire homes and farms, and by 1972, more than 200 families had been evicted. By 1984, more than 8,000 people had lost their homes. As support for the dam faded and the opposition grew, the Army Corps of Engineers decided to recoup some expenses by offering the now-vacant homes for rent. Advertisements were placed in the *Village Voice*, and its readers responded en masse.

Dubbed the Tocks squatters, these people moved to the Pennsylvania side of the river. Former residents of the vacated houses took exception and so did many area residents. Tension escalated into violent nighttime raids, where homes were burned and livestock was slaughtered. It seemed that history was repeating itself in the Delaware River valley.

The confrontations ceased when armed U.S. marshals made a raid of their own a few years later and escorted the squatters out of the valley. The Army Corps of Engineers moved swiftly, leveling many historic houses and outbuildings before a restraining order stopped them.

The final stages of the anti-dam movement came with the declaration of the Delaware River as a national wild and scenic river. The war in Vietnam was taking most of the funding, the environmental opposition was huge, and the dam site was judged unsafe. The dam idea waned, and the Army Corps of Engineers left the upper Delaware River valley. The Tocks Island dam project was not officially deauthorized until 1992.

For a small island, Tocks certainly caused a stir, becoming a household name to anyone living in or near the upper Delaware River valley in the 1960s. Tocks is an uninhabited, small island midstream in the Delaware River, about six miles north of the water gap. This photograph, from left to right starting at the lower left corner, shows Shawnee Island, Depue Island, Labar Island, and Tocks Island. (Courtesy of Casey Kays.)

The 1955 flood resulted from the effects of Hurricane Connie, which dumped about eight inches of rain in the Delaware River valley. That alone would not have been so bad, but Connie was followed by Hurricane Diane, and that was more than the river could take. Fed by overflowing tributaries, the Delaware River crested at 28 feet. The floods killed more than 200 people, including about 100 in the upper Delaware River region. Deaths in the upper valley were due to a 30-foot wall of water on the Brodhead Creek rather than from the Delaware River, but it was enough to spurn a renewed interest in damming the river. The 1955 flood gave the federal government a reason to become involved in the affairs of the upper Delaware River valley. (Courtesy of the Montague Association for Restoration and Community History.)

The old Milford bridge stood high above the river on sturdy stone supports. During the 1955 flood, the water covered the supports completely and lapped at the road surface. Residents watched and waited to see if the old bridge would be swept away again. The new Milford toll bridge was already in use high above the floodwaters. (Courtesy of the Montague Association for Restoration and Community History.)

In 1965, while the Tocks Island dam idea was very new, Glenn Fisher and Casey Kays began telling people about Sunfish Pond, a glacial lake on top of the mountain in the Worthington State Forest in New Jersey not far from the water gap. It seemed that a partnership of several different companies had quietly purchased Sunfish Pond and 708 acres from the State of New Jersey and were planning to build a pumped-water storage system. This plan would have destroyed the pond—something that was unacceptable to Fisher and Kays. The two men, along with Thomas Ritter, formed the Lenni Lenape League and began the fight to save Sunfish Pond. The fight for the pond became the first grassroots effort to have a major impact on future New Jersey conservation practices. (Courtesy of Casey Kays.)

Above (from left to right), Glenn Fisher, Thomas Ritter, and Casey Kays continued fighting for Sunfish Pond, and on Mother's Day in 1966, they held their first public event—a pilgrimage to the pond. It was to be one of many. In 1967, more than 600 people, led by Supreme Court justice William O. Douglas, marched to the pond in a highly publicized event. Conservationists in favor of saving Sunfish Pond were opposed to Tocks Island, and all of them called for deauthorization of the dam. Someone suggested that the Army Corps of Engineers turn its holdings over to the National Park Service, making the whole area a national park instead. (Courtesy of Casey Kays.)

In 1970, the Lenni Lenape League celebrated a victory as Sunfish Pond was declared a national landmark. Sunfish Pond was deeded back to the state as part of Worthington State Forest. Kays (at right) had succeeded in setting an example for other environmentalists. Sunfish Pond was safe for the moment, but a greater danger still loomed in the valley below. It was only natural that Sunfish Pond activists turned their attention to defeating the Tocks Island dam, joining forces with those already taking up the fight. Fisher even became one of the squatters in an effort to preserve some of the historic buildings, which ultimately failed. (Courtesy of Casey Kays.)

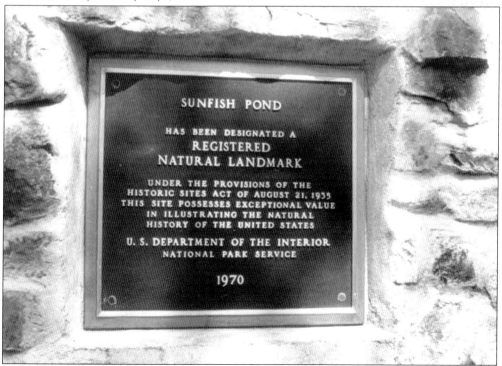

SUNFISH POND

HAS BEEN DESIGNATED A
REGISTERED
NATURAL LANDMARK

UNDER THE PROVISIONS OF THE
HISTORIC SITES ACT OF AUGUST 21, 1935
THIS SITE POSSESSES EXCEPTIONAL VALUE
IN ILLUSTRATING THE NATURAL
HISTORY OF THE UNITED STATES

U. S. DEPARTMENT OF THE INTERIOR
NATIONAL PARK SERVICE

1970

NO MORE SHAD,
OYSTERS, FARMS,
FORESTS...

EAT AN ENGINEER
FOR LUNCH, TOMORROW

NIX ON TOCKS

FUTURE POLLUTION LEVEL 430'

About the same time that Casey Kays, Glenn Fisher, and Thomas Ritter initiated the campaign to save Sunfish Pond, lifelong Minisink resident Nancy Shukaitis organized the first anti-Tocks movement in the Delaware River valley. With these two groups in the lead, the battle lines were drawn between the conservationists and the Army Corps of Engineers. Joan Matheson, another anti-Tocks activist, published the *Minisink Bull* newspaper to keep people informed about the activities of the Army Corps of Engineers and the politics around the dam controversy. Matheson was also well known for her signs. One, posted along her Dingmans Ferry property, read, "Welcome to Tax Island Dam Dollar-Wear National Wreck Area. You Pay Nature Staggers Industry Profits." The *Minisink Bull* also published reader suggestions for a new name for the proposed park. The favorites included Dollarwear National Pork, Sh——Creek (to immortalize the position of the inhabitants), and Credibility Gap. (Courtesy of the National Park Service.)

In 1971, the Army Corps of Engineers delayed groundbreaking for the dam while an environmental impact statement was prepared. Opposition was mounting, funds were coming up short, and, to add to the corps' misery, huge mistakes were being made. In an effort to rid the valley of squatters, an armed confrontation took place in February that finally removed the squatters from the historic houses they held. The corps's bulldozers moved in almost immediately, destroying several historic homes before they could be documented or anything of value could be salvaged. The corps then accelerated the razing of homes and farms, including the 1850s Farmington House (above) and the *c.* 1867 Valentine Weaver House (below), in an effort to keep other squatters from moving in. (Courtesy of the National Park Service.)

St. John's Episcopal Church, built around 1860 in Dingmans Ferry, was truly a unique building. It did not resemble any of the other churches and was described as being "country wooden gothic." The vertical board-and-batten siding, stained-glass windows, and steep gable roof made this church one of the more picturesque focal points of the village. The Army Corps of Engineers purchased and demolished this church as part of its preparations for the Tocks Island dam. (Courtesy of the National Park Service.)

In preparation for the dam construction, the Army Corps of Engineers had drilled an exploratory adit into the side of Kittatinny Mountain opposite the lower end of Tocks Island about 60 feet above the river. Over the years, additional core samples were also taken from Tocks Island itself and from the mountains where the dam would be anchored. To its dismay, the Army Corps of Engineers discovered that instead of there being a bedrock base under the Delaware River at the dam site, there was an unstable mixture of glacial till, drift, and alluvial deposits left from the last ice age and a geological fault line. This information, coupled with the enormous oppositions and lack of funding, signaled the beginning of the end for the Tocks Island dam. (Courtesy of Casey Kays.)

Before the bridges were built across the Delaware River, the major mode of transportation for many years was the ferryboats. Most of the ferryboats were very similar in construction, quite large and able to transport several horses, wagons, and automobiles. The Rosenkrans Ferry was one of the major ferry services in the early days of the upper Delaware River valley. The remains of the Rosenkrans Ferry sat for a long time on the edge of the river in Worthington State Forest. One of the VanCampen descendents had purchased the old ferry, hoping to use it to harvest hay from one of the islands. The ferry remained on the roadside until the state bulldozed it down the river embankment, shortly after this photograph was taken in 1976. (Courtesy of Casey Kays.)

The Peter Treible House, also called the Rouch House, was a beautiful example of an early stone house. A date stone on the southwest gable read 1832, with the initials P. T. This house was a few miles northeast of Shawnee on Delaware in Pennsylvania and had an interesting history. The house was the home of Treible but also served as the post office from 1843 to 1847 and for most of the 19th century was a popular tavern. The basement housed a unique compartment built into the stone wall that served as a cooling cellar, probably from its days as a tavern. The building was demolished by the Army Corps of Engineers. (Courtesy of the Library of Congress, Prints and Photographs Division.)

As the controversies over the dam lingered, the Army Corps of Engineers and, later, the National Park Service found themselves with a lot of vacant buildings and very little funding. When enthusiasm for the dam finally died out and the years passed by, buildings began to show signs of benign neglect. Sometimes a quick fix (above) postponed a building's demise for a short while, but for most of the homes and outbuildings that were not already demolished, it was—and still is—just a matter of time. (Courtesy of the National Park Service.)

Nine

RECREATION AREA

The federal government had undoubtedly created a very sticky situation in the upper Delaware River valley. Enforcing its right to eminent domain, the government had procured 70,000 acres of privately held properties in anticipation of the Tocks Island project. The park it had envisioned to maintain the lands surrounding a very big recreational lake became the obvious alternative for the reservoir that did not happen, and the DWGNRA came into being under the stewardship of the National Park Service.

It was a long and difficult road for the park service. In the minds of former residents, the park service was synonymous with the government and Army Corps of Engineers. There was much resentment and animosity still raging in the valley, and the relationship between the area residents and the park service was something comparable to that of the Lenapes and the English.

In all fairness to the park service, it suddenly found itself caretaker of a lot of historic houses that were supposed to be underwater. Understaffed and underfunded, community relations went from bad to worse as the remaining houses were boarded up and seemingly forgotten.

It has taken some time, but the park service has been working hard toward long-term goals for the DWGNRA even as the park has grown in popularity, with annual visits at nearly five million per year. Restoration projects, including more than $500,000 for the VanCampen Inn, have given new life to some of the most historic structures. Studies, surveys, and archaeological assessments have sorted the remaining properties into those that are worth saving, those that might be saved through cooperative efforts, and those that are beyond repair.

Relationships between the community and the park service are better now, and even the evicted residents can agree that if the DWGNRA was not here, the Delaware River valley might be covered by new developments. Perhaps it is time to learn from the Lenapes. It will be up to future generations to care for the land well and to preserve the history and wilderness of the Minisink.

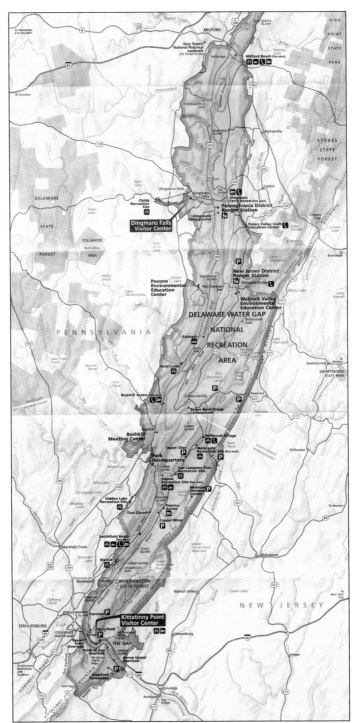

The DWGNRA spans 70,000 acres and almost 40 miles of the river in Pennsylvania and New Jersey. The National Park Service headquarters is in Bushkill, but there are ranger stations and visitor centers throughout the park. The DWGNRA is just over an hour's drive from the New York metropolitan area. (Courtesy of the National Park Service.)

112

Visitors entering the DWGNRA from metropolitan areas are amazed at the expanse of wilderness that lies within such a short drive from the cities. (Courtesy of Rob Socha.)

The National Park Service maintains wildlife management areas and natural areas, and wildlife in the park is plentiful. The park is a haven for birding and butterfly enthusiasts and attracts millions of wildlife watchers every year. (Courtesy of Rob Socha.)

Charles Peirce (pronounced "purse"), one of America's most well-known philosophers, lived in this house with his wife, Juliette, from 1887 until his death in 1914. Some of Peirce's most noted work was accomplished while living in the house they called Arisbe. Located near Milford, this house is now the home of the National Park Service Division of Research and Resource Planning. (Courtesy of the National Park Service.)

The park service restored the 1820s Neldon Roberts stone house in Montague, which for a time served as a school with living quarters for the schoolmaster on the second floor. The Montague Association for Restoration and Community History operates a museum in this building and in the Foster Armstrong House. (Courtesy of Rob Socha.)

Julius Foster purchased a tract of land on River Road (Old Mine Road) in 1791 and built the main part of the Foster Armstrong House. Foster learned about Dutch construction techniques while living on Long Island. The house reflects the Dutch influence in the gambrel roof and flare at the end-gable eve. When James Armstrong married Foster's daughter around 1812, they added the stone kitchen wing. Foster and son-in-law Armstrong operated a ferry from this site for many years. Enterprising businessmen, Foster and Armstrong also ran a store, a sawmill, a blacksmith shop, and a cider press on the property. The house was also a popular tavern and inn, providing overnight lodging for travelers on the Delaware River. (Courtesy of the National Park Service.)

The Foster Armstrong House remained in the Foster-Armstrong family, shown here in an undated family reunion, until purchased by the Army Corps of Engineers in 1970. The house stood vacant, with windows and doors boarded up, for many years. The park service later discovered that the intention to protect the houses by boarding them up was actually causing more deterioration. The boards prevented ventilation and light into the houses, encouraging mold, mildew, and peeling paint. The crowbars used to pry the securely nailed boards, whether by vandals or by the park service for interior surveys or maintenance, caused even more damage. The boarded-up look also invited vandalism. The window and door seals have since been improved on remaining houses, allowing ventilation and a certain amount of light inside. (Courtesy of the Montague Association for Restoration and Community History.)

The Foster Armstrong House features the Dutch gambrel roof and the Dutch kick on the eaves, designed to allow rainwater to roll out from the edge of the roof instead of down the walls. Gabled chimneys once served four corner fireplaces. The kitchen wing features a large cooking fireplace and a beehive oven. This house is unusual in that the large two-story portion was built first in 1720 as an addition to a smaller house on the site. The present kitchen wing was added sometime around 1812 and probably replaced the original small house. The Montague Association for Restoration and Community History, by special arrangement with the National Park Service, opens the Foster Armstrong House on Sundays during the summer months for its monthly meetings and for special events throughout the year. The association provides docents for the guided tours. The house is furnished with historical pieces from the 1700s through the early 1900s. (Courtesy of Rob Socha.)

At one time, the VanCampen Inn had a smaller wing attached. Opinions differ as to which part of the house was built first, but it is generally agreed that the smaller section was built in 1742 by Alexander Rosenkrans, who sold it to his brother-in-law Isaac VanCampen. VanCampen built the present section around 1754. The smaller section was removed or collapsed sometime around 1917. The stones were used to replace a wall in the Dutch barn and possibly to build a porch that was on the house when the Army Corps of Engineers acquired the building in 1970. Restoration began in 1984. After 230 years of the back hill pushing on the house, the stone wall had begun to bow and the foundation was crumbling. The National Park Service had to excavate under the house and stabilize the basement and rear wall of the building. (Courtesy of Tom Solon, National Park Service.)

Restoration of the VanCampen Inn was an engineering challenge. To preserve the structural integrity of the house while keeping the historical detail and accuracy, the 22-inch stone walls on the south side and most of the front had to be painstakingly removed. To passersby observing the scene, it was a marvel the building did not collapse. (Courtesy of Tom Solon, National Park Service.)

Interior walls and floors were finished to reflect their original condition whenever possible. Nailer blocks were placed in the stone wall so pegs could be added to hang clothes. The original interior walls were clay-lime plaster and lathe. Plaster was applied directly to the stonework on the exterior walls. Once the necessary stabilizations and restorations were complete, the walls were rebuilt with the original stones. (Courtesy of Tom Solon, National Park Service.)

The VanCampen Inn is the crown jewel of National Park Service restorations within the DWGNRA. The Walpack Historical Society, by special arrangement with the National Park Service, makes it possible for the inn to be open for public tours on alternate Sundays during the summer months. The historical society also helps to sponsor an annual VanCampen day, held each year in October. (Courtesy of Rob Socha.)

Dark forests, deep ravines, sparkling waterfalls, and endless stone rows through the woods are part of the landscapes within the park. Headstones are embedded in old trees, former basement holes are covered with vines and leaves, and a French and Indian War fort may be just around the corner. Nature lovers, hikers, bicyclists, birders, botanists, and, of course, history buffs find there are not enough hours in the day to enjoy all that there is to see. (Courtesy of Rob Socha.)

The legendary Old Mine Road, part of the "good road to Esopus," is still a dirt road in parts of its travels through Sussex County. Once not more than a rough wagon road, most of it is paved today. But here, in the most densely populated state in the country, lies a section of dirt road steeped in history. The town names have changed only slightly—Peters Valley was formerly called Bevans—but the way there is the same. (Above, courtesy of Rob Socha; below, author's collection.)

In spite of its dubious beginnings and the lingering bitterness from families who were ousted from their homes and farms, many people have come to have a better understanding of the dilemma of the National Park Service. Funding is almost nonexistent, so outside groups of interested people help to monitor the existing houses and attempt to raise money for others. While many historic houses have been lost forever, others are patiently awaiting restoration and a second lease on life. Time will tell whether these homes will also be restored and saved or will eventually fade into oblivion. (Courtesy of the National Park Service.)

People come from all over the world to canoe, kayak, raft, and fish the Delaware River. Wildlife abounds throughout the park, and one of the most numerous resident species is the black bear. People using the hiking and biking trails should obtain the bear-aware pamphlets that are available at visitor centers and ranger stations before venturing into the woods. (Courtesy of Rob Socha.)

Canoeists paddle past the end of Tocks Island. What most people have come to realize is that the events of the past have served a greater purpose in the end. As the Lenapes believed, people are caretakers of the land, not owners of the land. The presence of the National Park Service has saved the upper Delaware River valley from certain development. The wild and scenic Delaware River attracts more than five million visitors a year to this narrow bit of wilderness, and yet the land remains pristine and full of life. It is hoped that future generations of people will continue to paddle past Tocks Island on a warm summer day in awe of the undeveloped wilderness that is the heart of the DWGNRA. (Courtesy of Casey Kays.)

ACROSS AMERICA, PEOPLE ARE DISCOVERING SOMETHING WONDERFUL. *THEIR HERITAGE.*

Arcadia Publishing is the leading local history publisher in the United States. With more than 3,000 titles in print and hundreds of new titles released every year, Arcadia has extensive specialized experience chronicling the history of communities and celebrating America's hidden stories, bringing to life the people, places, and events from the past. To discover the history of other communities across the nation, please visit:

www.arcadiapublishing.com

Customized search tools allow you to find regional history books about the town where you grew up, the cities where your friends and family live, the town where your parents met, or even that retirement spot you've been dreaming about.